Signals

Signals

Ed Madden

Foreword by Afaa Weaver

THE UNIVERSITY OF SOUTH CAROLINA PRESS

Published in Cooperation with the South Carolina Poetry Initiative,
University of South Carolina

For Isabel —
Great to see you at the
SC festival ! ! Keep writing !
Ed Madden
19 May 2012

© 2008 University of South Carolina

Published by the University of South Carolina Press
Columbia, South Carolina 29208

www.sc.edu/uscpress

Manufactured in the United States of America

17 16 15 14 13 12 11 10 09 08   10 9 8 7 6 5 4 3 2 1

Library of Congress Cataloging-in-Publication Data

Madden, Ed, 1963–
    Signals / Ed Madden ; foreword by Afaa Weaver.
      p. cm. — (Winners of the South Carolina poetry book prize)
    Includes bibliographical references and index.
    ISBN 978-1-57003-750-4 (pbk : alk. paper)
    1. Southern States—Poetry. 2. Race—Poetry. I. Title.
PS3613.M2728S54 2008
    811'.6—dc22

                                                            2007043185

The South Carolina Poetry Book Prize is given annually to the manuscript that
wins the contest organized and sponsored by the South Carolina Poetry Initiative.
The winning title is published by the University of South Carolina Press in co-
operation with the South Carolina Poetry Initiative.

For Bert

How tenderly they must attend these friendships
or all is lost. All *is* lost.
Only the faithful hold this place green.
　　Robert Duncan, *The Opening of the Field*

Contents

III

Foreword

Signals combines a matter-of-fact lyrical eye with a view to harder social realities, and there is a consistency in the collection, a working with and around couplets and tercets, a sparseness that seems to match an arid landscape, a place where one searches for hope. This collection bears the evidence of a high level of craft alongside a concern for what goes on in our lives. "What treasures still lie beneath my feet?" the poet asks, avoiding the self-indulgent blind eye in favor of travel and seeking, traveling the past of the last half-century and traveling the present as it defies the past and the future. The voice here is an embodiment of hope, as in the lines from the poem "Auction" which sounds the word that names the collection "The air trembles with signals: the raised hand / averted glance . . . / / There are things, and there is the love of things."

AFAA WEAVER

Acknowledgments

Grateful acknowledgment is made to the editors of the follow-
ing publications in which these poems first appeared, some in
slightly different versions:

Arkansas Review: "Amagon, Arkansas"
James Dickey Newsletter: "Trough"
Recorder: Journal of the American Irish Historical Society:
    "At the Mütter Museum" and "Kilnaboy"
Solo: A Journal of Poetry: "Inventory"
South Carolina Review: "Molasses"
Southern Humanities Review: "Auction"
White Crane: "Flaneur"

Several of the poems in this book, especially the final section,
were published in the chapbook *Signals* (2006), winner of the
South Carolina Poetry Initiative's inaugural chapbook contest in
2005. "Sunday Morning, Wadmalaw" also appears in *The Seagull
Reader: Poems* (2007). "Cabin near Caesar's Head" appears in *The
Southern Poetry Anthology: South Carolina* (2007).

I am grateful to the South Carolina National Heritage
Corridor and the South Carolina Poetry Initiative, which spon-
sored a residency at Fort Moultrie in 2005, and to the South
Carolina State Park System, for which I served as an artist in resi-
dence in 2006. A very special thanks goes to Carlin Timmons
and the staff at Fort Moultrie National Park on Sullivan's Island

and to the staff at Keowee-Toxaway State Park, where many of these poems were conceived or written.

I am grateful to my first teachers, Judith Kroll, David Wevill, and Tom Whitbread, and to Rafael Campo and that extraordinary 1997 workshop in Key West. I am also grateful to Afaa Michael Weaver for his selection of this book. Special thanks also are owed to Jack Brannon, Gordon Grant, Etta Madden, and Ray McManus; to the members of the First Book Project workshop group, as well as Nathalie Anderson and the ACIS poets; and to Bert Easter, first and dearest reader.

Very special thanks go to Mike Williams, whose work I have long admired, for the image that graces the cover of this book.

And to Kwame Dawes, my deepest gratitude.

I

Trough

Cowlake, Arkansas, 1969

For the horses, in the run between the barn and the pasture,
where a catalpa tree bears its crop of worms. What draws you?

Constant tug of the dark water, the still water, its insides
tin and slick with green. Almost as tall as you are and—

your cousin warns—big enough to drown in. Just inside
the barbed wire that snags you when you lean over to stir

the darkness, to stare at the fish, enormous fish in the
    dark water,
gold and black, rising like apparitions to the surface,

where you scatter oatmeal stolen from your grandma's
    cupboards,
an offering, a secret. The fish come to you, bidden, hungry.

They are everywhere. They are always hungry.

Silver

at Lake Keowee, early spring

The long white leaves of the switch cane litter
the path like the shed petals of a winter flower.

Last night's geese are gone, the valley quiet.
The sky is milk. The setting sun is cold and white,

the kingfisher a blue missile, iridescent.
We toss crumbs from the dock, bits of biscuit,

and swirls of perch churn the green water.
Near the shore, the water is so still and clear

white shells gleam on the red mud.
The rhododendrons have begun to bud,

but still lift the dry brown stars of last year's
blooms. By evening, the lake is a plate of silver.

What I Found

Keowee-Toxaway State Park, March 2006

I

How long can you stare at the lake?
How long can you stare at the sky?

A boat's wake massages the shore.

In the sand, driftwood, limbs
and roots worn smooth, numb.

Take the largest piece you can
carry back to the cabin.

Place it on the porch like a totem.

II

A small black conical shell, splinter the water left.

Alder cones, resurrection plant, the dried pipsissewa.
A merkin of moss.

A scorpion, tail raised in threat, dry and dead,
near the cabin door.

A branch of forsythia in bloom, placed
in a dark olive wine bottle.

A little red rubber fish: child's toy, evidence.

III

The windows are dark. The light makes a circle
of mossy lawn just beyond the door.

On the radio someone sings, *Who says you can't go home?*
I haven't spoken to my father in a decade.

The lake is a darkness behind the night's darkness.
The rain isn't here yet, but will be soon.

Self-Portrait with Lettered Olives

Folly Beach, South Carolina

To bend is to gather the small shells, gold
hoard, your fingers stiff in the cold surf,

the lettered olives rolling on the sand—
a delta of shell, elegant dosinias crushed

to bits, coquinas, spiraled augers. To list them
is like saying a spell: moon snail, baby's ear,

pen shell, nutmeg, incongruous ark, conch
or whelk, and this handful of lettered olives.

This one was orange, was wet, smelled of salt,
smelled of death rolled up inside—now

of nothing, the orange gone brown, a cone
of russet and white, the lip of shell thick

and notched, tiny hieroglyphs of damage
and sand. What was once alive is dead,

what was golden is now burnished to bone.

Tansy

A black lacquered box gleams on the shelf,
a sheen almost wet among the dusty objects,

tschotkes, wall pockets, ceramic bowls.
It's shellacked in tansies, yellow flowers etch

the box like lace, languid, almost Asian, aesthetic.

In the bad soil of the backyard, it spreads,
takes over the yarrow, coreopsis, calendula, even

the bronze fennel. It escapes the bed we make,
worse than wisteria—everywhere the ferny leaves, the bitter

buttons of yellow, pungent, lacelike, abortifacient.

Kilnaboy

Ireland, May 2006

The students gather in the green church,
the old walls covered in moss and briar,

the roof a cold blue sky. Gravestones,
littered with plastic roses, mostly faded,

tumble beyond the empty doorway. Looking
back as we leave, we see her above the door—

Sheela-na-gig, grey ghost of the transom,
witch on the wall—obscene, riveting, her genitals

a worn cleft. Not worth the trip,
someone mutters, and we amble back to the bus,

headed to lunch, to Poulnabrone.
At the dolmen tomb, the wind is cold,

and we huddle for photos. In the cracks
of this limestone moonscape, in the moist grikes

all around us, there are ferns, gentians,
the lurid purple spikes of early orchids.

Variations on a Postcard, Achill Island, 1960s

I

A boy in a blue jumper walks in the road.
Three girls penned behind a wire fence, whispering.

Above the mountain, a sea made of sky,
and in the west an island of cloud split

by the power line that spans the card—
as if a fifth of it were severed from the rest.

The road is freshly tarred for the photograph.
The road vanishes in a small town.

II

Scalloped edges suggest something fancy—
something to send to a friend in the States.

A power line bisects the card, and the streetlamp
soars above Slievemore like the myth of a new nation.

Three girls sit behind the fence, cooped up.
Three boys walk the road—one headed into town,

the others walking out, headed out to Keem Bay,
one carrying a white sack full of what he needs.

III

The houses are white, surrounded by walls
of white stucco or stacked black rock, save one

in front circled by a wire fence stretched
around wooden posts, three girls inside.

One of the girls wears a red dress.
The power line is a scrawl across the card.

The boy wears a blue jumper—blue like the sky,
blue like the two cars parked along the road,

blue being the color of elsewhere.

II

Inventory

The Audubon prints, the English china,
the flamingo painting, the lacquer trays—

several lists of Sam's possessions
lie on the table of his former lover—

a sewing machine, the Soloflex,
imported sweaters, a box of books,

the chifforobe, large and ornate,
heavy wood of a polished coffin.

Each page has a name at the top of a list.
The elder brother, who hopes to close

the affair soon, is recipient of Sam's
collection of monkeys, decorated boxes,

an ebony bowl. The sister rejects
the bedroom suite, the princess dresser,

the wardrobe and all that he has left her
(though not the clothes she's already taken).

She wants the green sofa, will have
nothing else. So strange the way

grief is manifested as greed.
No one claimed the porn: it disappeared

the day of the funeral. Sam hoped
to curse his lover with joy, left him

the boxes of holiday ornaments, though
the sister must have those things, too,

stores them now with the Empire chairs,
the gazing globe, blue as a bruise.

To others he leaves the Polynesian figures,
the end table shaped like an Indian slave,

who holds a platter of glass on his head—
he kneels to offer a collection of snapshots,

ex-lover and friends in Halloween drag
(pirate, vampire, courtesan, queen),

and a framed photo of San Francisco,
a bridge spanning waves of fog,

and paradise on the other side, waiting,
the streets of gold, the gates of pearl.

Auction

The air trembles with signals: the raised hand,
averted glance, the hover over laden tables.

There is the love of things and there are all
the minor perversions, strange desires and addictions:

devotees of Weller and Van Briggle, lovers
of Mission style, the fainting couch, the slave

chair, a finger lingering on lip of bowl,
tracing needs as palpable as porcelain.

The auctioneer begins his chant, his assistant
lifts the Tiffany vase, a Griswold skillet,

and the pottery—Camark, Niloak, Fulper, Grueby,
Newcomb, Jugtown, Roseville, Pisgah Forest—

in the music of a name an aura glows, material
transformed as if by magic into something more

than merely history, more than sentimental.
There are things, and there is the love of things.

We attend the auctions, raise our bids, vaguely
aware of the difference between exchange and use

value—the depression glass in which we serve
sherbert, savor the tang of raspberry or peach

melting against the shimmer of green glass.

Blue

A coy moon glows beyond
swags of moss, streaks of blue

underglaze dangling from dark
blue limbs of cypress trees.

The swamp is a wash of blue fog
around the base of a Newcomb vase.

Look closer: a blue house
daubed on the swamp's blue shore,

where a man sleeps
in cobalt dark, a man

with a white face, coy hands
blue in the room's shadows,

in the blue and humid air.
A vase glows on the oak

sideboard, dark blue luster—
something he might use,

were it not for the blue
night, the blue sky,

the glaze of dark blue trees.

Emblem

My favorite find is a hand-tinted print
from a series of biblical subjects, my heart

set on one: Lot's family fleeing Sodom,
orange flames on the far horizon,

two beautiful angels in long robes and
cerulean wings, leading them out of the end

of things. Adrift, far from home, we sing
old hymns, claim the emblems of family,

other people's heirlooms—the horsehair sofa,
deathbed daguerreotypes, emblems of the way

things might have been, the image of a city
burning, a family fleeing, and Lot's wife

turning, not yet salt, just a misgiving.

Flaneur

for Bert

Wandering through Les Puces de Paris Saint-Ouen—
the world's biggest flea market, your guidebook said—

I stop to finger through a box of cufflinks.
It's difficult to find a pair, all buttons and studs.

In my pocket, a rock from Wilde's grave,
something to remember a summer afternoon

of strolling the cobbled paths among the tombs.
I linger over red glass, pearl and bone.

You wander on, pausing at a shelf of pottery,
lifting a pearlescent jar in the afternoon sun,

the base blue, the crystalline glaze like ice,
like prisms in the hot August light.

You wait on me for the inevitable haggling—
my college French working well enough,

though it failed us at the bar, where pickpockets
lifted a wad of francs from your jeans.

The way things end—all our bohemian dreams—
you take a torn bag to wrap them up

and tuck the cufflinks safely in the jar.

At the Mütter Museum

Philadelphia, 2004

The display cases along the rail are filled
with images of conjoined twins—some
have two heads, others only one.

There are no pictures of their mothers,
just newspaper clippings, fetuses in jars,
plastic models. We circle the atrium, peering

over the bank of display cases and down
into the gallery of medical oddities. The steps
down are steep, and the place is filled with children—

more vocal and honest about their disgust
and pleasure than we are. There are wax models
of skin diseases, eyeballs pierced by splinter

or clouded over with disease. Children whir
through the room, fascinated by syphilitic sores,
the enormous gangrenous intestine, jars

of deformities, babies born with their organs
outside their bodies. The tour guide's voice
is a low hum in the corner, reasonable and sure.

Two boys in front of me shriek with pleasure
at something preserved in formaldehyde. I look
across the room at you, you smile, and some

visceral understanding—like a cord
across the room—tightens between us.

Home Economics

Fairview Drive was dark with ivy, hostas
shining in every yard, and beneath it all

the insistent drone of roots and stems, the hum
of things thickening—that dark industry beneath

our feet. That afternoon, we made gin
and tonics—wanted *caipirinhas,* but didn't

have *cachaças* or lime. "You just can't
make a good cocktail if you don't

know a foreign language," Bert said.
"It's trinkle-down economics." He began

to sing, something I barely heard, stacking
the azalea's severed limbs at the curb.

Tu lo sai quanto t'amai. The flowerbeds
glittered with weeds, and here and there, evening

daubed the street with sweetness, four-o'clocks opening,
and then the jimson, heady and white, dandelions

scattered like lint across the lawns.

Cabin near Caesar's Head

for Rod and Ed, October 2005

The moon is luminous. We sit quiet
on the back porch. To the north,
Brevard, the cabin's front yard
a valley of lights; to the south

Caesar's Head, the Devil's Kitchen—
that cold cleft in the mountain
where we'd stopped only hours before—
and the dark valleys of South Carolina.

The leaves aren't turning yet, the summer
too dry—only the sassafras and sumac,
gold and red, and a bruise of dogwood
at the front door. The Joe Pye weed

towers over Slick Rock Drive,
here, just off See Off Mountain Road.
A dead copperhead lies coiled in the road.
A woodpecker, tentative, tests a tree.

They've had the cabin for years. They tell us
stories of storms, Hurricane Ivan—
even here, so high—ripping off
the screen porch. Lightning, rattlesnakes,

a forest fire only yards away.
The eerie quiet when the valleys fill
with clouds. Quiet now, four men
talking quietly beneath the moon.

There's a kind of openness here—
it's not the vodka tonics or the moon—
just the way two men may be
together. They made themselves a place.

We visit the falls. Ed stops,
can't make the long walk,
and Rod heads back at the first falls.
We stand in the spray, thanking them.

The roads are lined with sumac and aster,
the shadows filled with galax, coltsfoot,
the small flowers of the closed gentian—
lilac and white, bloom that won't open.

The guidebook says they're rare, but here
they are. Bees force their way
into the blooms. The road is dark.
The ferns turn golden in the sun.

Spider Lilies

In fall, when hurricanes approach the coast,
they rise, quickly, above the beds—*lycoris,*

spider lilies, hurricane lilies, the red
sheaths peeling back like a kind of need,

bright spangles of blossom among the dying
and spent. This late urge for color surprises

us; the frail curls of petal, sprays of anther
claim our attention. The rains will batter

the garden soon, but for now I water, dazed
by these burning flowers, these hands raised—

raised and trembling in late September's warm
vespers, these livid, tender welts of joy.

III

Here, or the White Boy on the Bus

We need, in every community,
a group of angelic troublemakers.
                    Bayard Rustin, September 1963

You put together the whole thing, Mr. March—
1963, the year I'm born, Bayard—

with no cell phone, no email, no fax, just
that stack of 3x5 cards in your back pocket.

You Quaker, socialist, pacifist, activist,
you spent three years in prison to protest war.

Brother Outsider, a chain gang convict
arrested a decade before Rosa Parks

for refusing to move to the back
of the bus—you pointed at a white kid

sitting nearby, said, *If I move, this child*
will not know that injustice is taking place

here. Strom Thurmond pilfered your past
to try to stop the March—1953 arrest

in Pasadena, a black man in the back
of a car with two other men, cited

for sexual perversion. J. Edgar slipped
Thurmond the dirt—in Hoover's house

are many closets, garters and daughters—
which Thurmond inserted into Congressional

Record, reading in salacious detail the tale
of your arrest, *a known homosexual*.

The March went on, as did you.

I dream I am that white boy on the bus,
your finger pointing at me. I watch

the police lift you from your seat—
Bayard, black angel, troublemaker—

force you to the street. The bus pulls away,
folks turn back to their business,

a white man takes the seat, looks at
that boy, wondering what he knows.

Confederates

going north on I-95, March 2000

Bert stops at the BP for gas.
I go in for coffee while he pays.
He's fixing to say something, but doesn't—
the television above us stops him,
a man with a flag saying: *Learn your history.*
You better learn real history.

After the march, a woman asked us: *Where you from?*
Meaning, why are nice young men like you
marching with *them,* the river of black folk
purling around us, the flag
a bright flame in the cold sky.

Early March and we watch the road unfurl
behind us. We tell each other stories:
only boys when it all happened—
that bus full of kids overturned
by a white mob on a Darlington County road,
or that girl in Arkansas, escorted into school with guns.

To us, that flag's just something to do
with Lynyrd Skynyrd, old pickup trucks,
guys with long hair and tight jeans.

A gray fog haunts the highway.
Bert adjusts the rearview mirror.
Our friends are waiting at the next exit.

Signals

Fort Moultrie, January 2005

Four white ibis hunch on the yardarm—
the naval signal flags long gone—

just four white birds, their beaks tucked,
the winter sun cold and bright,

the fort's one flag snapping in the wind.

On the beach, sandpipers test the surf's edge,
pick through the detritus of tourist and tide.

You point to the dolphin out in the channel,
beyond it Fort Sumter, distant ruin.

Black breakers reach like arms out into the rough water.

In the parking lot, we smell the marsh beyond us,
and the sweetness of a tea olive nearby.

A bare tree suddenly blossoms in blackbird—
strange fruit shining in the morning sun.

A sulfur butterfly blows across the lawn.

Journal

*adapted from the camp diary of Thomas Wentworth
Higginson, December 1862*

As winter advances, butterflies gradually disappear.

One species (a *Vanessa*) lingers; three others
have vanished since I came. The colored people all say

that it will be much cooler, but my officers
do not think so, perhaps because last winter

was so unusually mild—with only one frost, they say.

Last night the water froze in the adjutant's tent,
but not in mine. To-day has been mild and beautiful.

The blacks say they do not feel the cold
so much as the white officers do, and perhaps it is so.

Beside the superb branch of uneatable bitter oranges
which decks my tent-pole,

I have to-day hung up a long bough of finger-sponge,
which floated to the riverbank.

∞

Many things glide by without the time to narrate them.

∞

I should think the colored people would suffer
and complain these cold nights; but they say nothing,

though there is a good deal of coughing.

I should fancy that the scarlet trousers must do something
to keep them warm, and wonder that they dislike them

so much, when they are so much like their beloved fires.

They certainly multiple firelight in any case.

I often notice that an infinitesimal flame,
with one soldier standing by it,

looks like quite a respectable conflagration.

Molasses

Fort Moultrie, February 2005

I

White tunnels draw us into the fort—
dull color of stucco, color of bone—

the walls bruised yellow where crews
mark the crumbling stucco for restoration.

The first color was onion, yellow onion
the pigment of ochre wash on old walls.

At the tunnel near the postern gate,
the grout has been gouged out between

the old bricks, bricks Anderson touched
as his men left in silence for Sumter,

their boats hidden beyond the rocks.
One tunnel ends in a locked gate.

The ranger tells me another was filled in
when the ruins became a national park.

The way it is with stories: the locked gate.
The way it is with history: the dark tunnel.

II

Carlin, the ranger, tells me the small building
that looks like a prison is the powder magazine,

barrels stacked beyond the barred door.
The chalky wash on the walls—color of sulfur,

color of pollen—is made with molasses.
The black sweetness thickens the mix of water

and lime. Sometimes, if the tide is low,
the water clear, you can still see

the palmetto cribbing, rotten thatch of history
beneath the beach. The air of closed tunnels

is dark and quiet. A coherent story requires
some gates be locked. What passages

still lie beneath the mud? Would I know
where to kneel and dig? Who first covered

the fort's walls with molasses and lime?
What treasures still lie beneath my feet?

Pest Houses, Sullivan's Island

In the stillness I see the things that are
not visible.

Marjory Wentworth, "Sand"

I

The houses are filled with phantoms.
Nothing remains. There is nothing physical here.

No eyewitness accounts describe what went on
in the pest house, *lazaretto.*

We don't know, exactly, where they stood,
small houses of wood, nothing left of them.

What tell-tale markers lie beneath the soil—
broken bottle, bits of bone, links of chain?

Bodies burned to ash, the dust we breathe.

Beneath what modern cottage? Beyond what street?

In the old documents, there are only
demands for new houses—the old ones already lost

in the recording, replaced, destroyed
by negligence, by hurricane.

(The houses moved across the harbor
when Charlestonians summering in Sullivan's heat

grew uncomfortable—death down the street,
disease in the breeze of myrtle and salt.)

Nothing physical remains, no foundation
of wood and sand, no map of the place.

Except I put my hand—

How, in the absence of the thing—

II

Only this: a bronze plaque,
a little out of the way, something you'd drive by—

historical marker for a battlefield, a ruin,
a place where something happened—

but this sign marks no place,
spectral houses of pestilence

rising everywhere on this four-mile island
of sand, sweet myrtle and beach homes.

Or this: the ritual, someone wades in the water—

the water here is powerful.

Pour the libations, rinse the cut
flowers with seawater—the salt of blood

stiffens the saltier oblivion of the sea.
Scatter the blossoms in the cove,

remember the unnamed, unnumbered dead.

Spectral houses line the shore.

Or this: a thing made out of words—

The place rumord to have been a House surely was.

III

There is nothing here—cold water, white sand,
a scattering of bone-white shells.

The water is powerful here.

Cut flowers are floating in the cove.

Sunday Morning, Wadmalaw

for Teresa and Fred, June 1998

I

The way the day began: a white sun, white sky,
the chatter and prattle of martins a kind of artless
    consecration

for the dawn. The guests woke slowly, each in turn; some
huddled over rituals of coffee, one wandered down the dirt
    path

to mass, others out to the dock, where I waited, expectant,
for the slow apparition of a white heron, flying

out of the sun. On such days, we reach for metaphor,
    something
to represent the way two people may decide to be

together. And so I waited on the deck for the white bird,
    before
it became a bird or white or near. Floral pediments from
    the wedding

remained on the porch, small towers of sunflower, palmetto,
    fern—
and vervain from the island's fields, a bloom like purple ash.

II

The bride waited at the end of a corridor of moss-draped oak,
her neck thin and graceful as the heron's, and nothing fragile

about her smile. She tossed her bouquet of magnolia into
   the river,
where it floated, only to be rescued later by a nephew

when it reached the muddy shore, the return of something
too beautiful to happen only once, as if every trajectory

had its return, every prodigal his home. Told he was next
to marry, the nephew threw it back to the tides, the
   deepening dark.

III

Photos capture an evening disappearing: her parents leaning
into a whisper; his parents leading a line dance; the beauty

of a man, barefoot and tan, whose slate-blue shirt echoed
    the hue
of his eyes; the quiet groom, the shining bride—memory an
    album

of nameless faces, an index of images and scents—mango
    cocktails
late in the evening, the dock moving beneath me like a lover.

IV

I broke a bloom of vervain to take home—its purple tipped
with a speck of blue, the color of the sky the morning after

the wedding, a cloudless blue lightening to white at the
    horizon.
The tide dawdled along the dock, the purple martins
    dithering,

a screen door slammed, the air was bright and hot, and not
prepared for anything—other than the bride and groom's
    expected visit

to say goodbyes—and then the surprise of the white heron
flying slowly from the sun, white on white, followed

moments later by another, a reply, the repetition
required by fate, and perhaps I thought—or hoped—its mate.

Coastal

Wadmalaw, summer 2004

Tall grass rustles along the creek,
the brown water slackens in the heat.

I walk a curve of shore where the grass
thins, and the ground stirs—tiny crabs,

fiddlers, grey as hardened mud. They skitter
sideways, claws raised. The ground is riddled

with burrows, claws extruding. The claw comes out
first—an attitude. Lights come on in the house

behind me. I lift a crab shell, cracked open,
sun-bleached chitin, its ridges crisp and unbroken,

dry husk of history, the inside still pearlescent.
My step raises a hundred claws of threat.

A stomp sends them scuttling thru the grass.
I imagine crushing one—the crunch of carapace,

small gush of guts in my fist. And if
I dropped it in the dark, others would find it,

their claws tugging at bits of brother meat.

Three Poems on Politics

I. Caucus

   for Becci, at Penn Center, Beaufort

As the evening speeches lengthened,
she looked out the long windows.

Inside the scrape of chairs, thick smell
of burnt coffee, fans beating the heavy air.

Outside, light swabbed the live oak leaves.
They looked wet, there, shining in the darkness.

II. Song

  for Bert, at Middleton Plantation

You went for a walk alone, along the trail
behind the conference hall, a warm morning
in February. Nothing was in bloom, you said,
nothing—too early still, even here.

Yet across the river were shivers of pink
azalea tipped with tight buds, attendant,
on paths mapping the old plantation, blisters
of blossom along the road, around the ruins.

No, nothing in bloom here, you said,
but the trees were full of birdsong, filling
the green and empty air, tendrils of song
spreading over the black, still water,

music you carried back into the meetings,
like a memory, the promise of what might be.

III. Transom

   for Jim Campbell

A vase of tulips gleams—pink
anomalies on a table filled with tracts.

The question that we're sniffing toward,
said the old black man, *is this:*

Can capitalism reform itself?
The window above the door is dark—

a thin transparent film to screen
the light. The sun is bright outside.

The clouds boil in slow swirls.

Amagon, Arkansas

after David Baker

Small towns puncture the highways leaving
Newport, the county seat, their smallness a kind
of grace. Everything has been left out

to weather—a car on blocks, rocking horse
faded to dusty blue. Driving through
is the prevailing point of view. There is

a portable sign in front of the store, where
the specials every day are staples: bread,
milk, ground chuck, and what's not advertised—

Shirley's crafts scattered across the shelves
on the back wall, Wayne's take on the weather.
There are stacks of snuff and Skoal cans

at the register. A box beneath the counter
has all the tabs, credit where credit is due.
Across the street at church, sermons rarely

leave casualties. Attendance is the only virtue
left; gossip and family take care of other
sins. Once a train ran through town,

but now just tractors and plows, pickup trucks
on the way to Wal-Mart, the big stores in Newport.
Or the John Deere dealer in Weiner, where

they have the rice festival every year,
cooking contests and beauty queens, harvest
longings transliterated as civic pride. Nothing

is lonelier here than attention. This is the season
when crop dusters are blamed for everyone's dying gardens.

Roots: An Essay on Race

It isn't bravery that's required
to watch a television
. . . .

Say No
to this only way they want to know Black people
                              Nikky Finney, "Pluck"

I am trying to say something about an ignorant
white kid, somewhere in the South in the seventies.

His dad is a farmer, raises rice and soybeans.
They have many farmhands, black and white.

His uncle yells, "Niggers in the back,"
when they load up the trucks in the fields

to head home. He sees Hiram Dean clench
his teeth, squeeze himself into the front cab.

His mom teaches him not to use the n-word.
What does he know of black people?

His first black teacher—Ms. Armitage,
fourth grade science—tells him she played baseball

with his uncles in lower Cowlake—the black
and white kids together on summer afternoons.

I am trying to say something about an ignorant
but good-hearted white boy in rural Arkansas.

His class is one of the first integrated
at Newport High—new port on the White River,

the trains for grain changing the map,
upriver, Jacksonport abandoned to its courthouse,

its gazebo, its fancy riverboat docked for tours,
stories of fresh-water pearls pulled from the muck.

With dad and brother, he catches catfish
in the muddy Cache. They fish the stocked pond,

throw back the trash fish, the gar on the line—
take a bucket of perch to Elsie and Kissie,

who live at the end of a dirt road
at the edge of the Epps farm, on Coon Island—

is that name still listed on the maps?

I am trying to say something about being

a naïve white boy, who attends an all-white
kindergarten, an all-white elementary (except

for Mary Charcia Birdsong, who rides his bus)—
until they move from Beedeville to Coon Island,

landing in the better school district.
What does he know of black people, other

than farmhands and Elsie and Kissie,
and *Roots* on TV. His parents, who protect

him from television—no *Happy Days,* no *All
in the Family,* no *Dark Shadows*—let him watch

the week of *Roots* with his little brother,
though they miss part of Sunday and Wednesday

nights, church nights. I am trying to say something
about being a white boy who leaves his white church

to hurry home to watch *Roots,* where he learns
of slavery and miscegenation, stories brutal but

sentimental. He is ignorant, he is so entranced
that when his father's Labrador retriever,

Sheba Shadow, gives birth to her first pups,
he thinks to name them for names memorized

from the miniseries—considers Toby
and Kizzy, Chicken George, Kunte Kinte.

How can he tell this story now?
Such names in the American Kennel Club

registry would look racist—maybe not
Black Jack, Ebony Mandy, or Storm,

but Toby Reynolds, Kunte Kinte's new name.
He knows his distant relatives, the Gradys,

don't let their black field hand eat at their table—
though they take him with them to the hill cabin

to cook their meals on the grill outside.
He sees his mother set a place for Nigger Roy.

Years later, he will rent a home from Talbert,
who calls his elder black employee "the boy."

Years later, he will march in honor of MLK.
But at that moment, there on the floor

of the mudroom, where Shadow has given birth
to seven shining black pups, what names

does he name, claiming Toby for his own?

I am trying to say something about being

that very boy, ignorant, good-hearted, and poor,
in love with the lineage and language of *Roots*.

He knows the rumor—that the grave at the back
of the family cemetery is that of a black man

who passed for white. The leaning stone
is weathered smooth, falling against

the barbed wire fence. Years later, home
from college, he and his father will visit

the home of Elsie and Kissie—deserted,
their children long gone. Mulberries will claim

the yard, honeysuckle and trumpet vine
the western porch. They will wander

the warm rooms—an abandoned chair, jars
on a sill. They will hear the growing hum

of bees inside the walls, and they will leave
quickly, stung—Jesus still pale and praying,

on the faded flue-plate hanging on the kitchen wall.

Dialectics

Just as history is never over
or complete, some conflicts can't be
reconciled, transcended, folded

into some higher, nobler thing.
The dry yard darkens with rain,
with all you wish you'd said

to the one inside, still sleeping.
Pollen scums the porch, sticks
to your bare feet. Nothing moves.

Rites

Leave now the locked gate, the crumbling wall.
Toss your offering in the cold waters of the cove.

The place rumord to have been the House surely was.

Set a table for the living and the dead,
the bowl of golden rice: stories in the grain.

Turn your eyes to the immoderate past.

Try to find the word—the blossom,
the offering, the rite—the thing that will suffice.

Borrow sacred devices. Smuggle the stories.
Swallow the seed, precious cargo. Weep.

In Key West, a Japanese poet gives me
the daruman doll, a Weeble with white eyes.

Color one eye, he says, *make your wish.*

The one-eyed doll stares from the shelf.

There are so many stories of loss.
The bowl of golden rice: my father.

In March, we will deck the church in lilies—
stargazer, calla—orchids, bells of Ireland.

Compose a song: song of *gailliardia,*
the island flower, song of the cordgrass,

song of spartina, myrtle and palm—
something, you might say, *like gratitude.*

Leave the fort for the open shore.
Press feet into wet sand: a kind of history.

Notes

The epigraph is from Robert Duncan's "This Place Rumord to Have Been Sodom," from *The Opening of the Field* (1960).

"*Here,* or the White Boy on the Bus" is deeply indebted to *Brother Outsider,* a documentary film about the life of Bayard Rustin. The epigraph comes from a speech Rustin gave on September 25, 1963, at the Community Church in New York, N.Y., entitled "After the March, What?" The speech was recorded and aired by Pacifica Radio and included in the audio track of *Brother Outsider.*

"Confederates"—In 1970 a mob of white protestors in Lamar, South Carolina, overturned a school bus of black children on its way to the newly integrated public school. The Confederate flag was removed from the dome of the South Carolina capitol on July 1, 2000. Earlier that year, on January 17 (Martin Luther King Day), almost fifty-thousand people rallied against the flag in a march on the statehouse grounds.

"Journal" adapts lines from the diaries of Thomas Wentworth Higginson, white colonel of the First Carolina Volunteers, a black regiment of the Army of the United States during the Civil War. The diaries were published in 1870 as *Army Life in a Black Regiment.*

The epigraph to "Pest Houses, Sullivan's Island" is taken from the poem "Sand," by Marjory Wentworth, from her book *Despite Gravity.*

"Molasses" was written after reading "Kiva Floor at Abo" by Ray Gonzalez.

Some lines in "Pest Houses, Sullivan's Island" and "Rites" are adapted from Allen Tate's "Ode to the Confederate Dead" and from Robert Duncan's "This Place Rumord to Have Been Sodom." "Rites" also adapts lines from "Thelma's Precious Cargo" and "Love Oil" by Kwame Dawes.

"Three Poems on Politics"—Penn Center, an African-American educational center established early in the Civil War, has served as an important site for community organizing.

"Transom"—When W. E. B. DuBois applied for membership in the Communist Party USA in 1961, he wrote in an open letter, "Capitalism cannot reform itself; it is doomed to self-destruction. No universal selfishness can bring social good to all."

The epigraph to "Roots: An Essay on Race" comes from Nikky Finney's "Pluck," from *Rice*.

Printed in the United States
109566LV00002B/55-171/P

9 781570 037504